LIFE
Lessons

WITH MAX LUCADO

BOOK OF ACTS

CHRIST'S CHURCH
IN THE WORLD

MAX LUCADO

Prepared by

THE LIVINGSTONE CORPORATION

THOMAS NELSON
Since 1798

NASHVILLE   DALLAS   MEXICO CITY   RIO DE JANEIRO   BEIJING

Life Lessons with Max Lucado—Book of Acts

Copyright © by Thomas Nelson, 2007

Pulished in Nashville, Tennessee. Thomas Nelson is a trademark of Thomas Nelson, Inc.

Thomas Nelson, Inc. titles may be purchased in bulk for educational, business, fundraising, or sales promotional use. For information, please email SpecialMarkets@ThomasNelson.com.

Produced with the assistance of the Livingstone Corporation (www.livingstonecorp.com). Project staff include Jake Barton, Joel Bartlett, Andy Culbertson, Mary Horner Collins, and Will Reaves

Editor: Neil Wilson

Cover Art and Interior Design by Kirk Luttrell of the Livingstone Corporation
Interior Composition by Rachel Hawkins of the Livingstone Corporation

ISBN-10: 1-4185-0945-0

ISBN-13: 978-1-4185-0945-3

Printed in the United States of America.

09 10 11 12 WC 18 17 16 15 14

HOW TO
STUDY THE BIBLE

This is a peculiar book you are holding. Words crafted in another language. Deeds done in a distant era. Events recorded in a far-off land. Counsel offered to a foreign people. This is a peculiar book.

It's surprising that anyone reads it. It's too old. Some of its writings date back five thousand years. It's too bizarre. The book speaks of incredible floods, fires, earthquakes, and people with supernatural abilities. It's too radical. The Bible calls for undying devotion to a carpenter who called himself God's Son.

Logic says this book shouldn't survive. Too old, too bizarre, too radical.

The Bible has been banned, burned, scoffed, and ridiculed. Scholars have mocked it as foolish. Kings have branded it as illegal. A thousand times over the grave has been dug and the dirge has begun, but somehow the Bible never stays in the grave. Not only has it survived; it has thrived. It is the single most popular book in all of history. It has been the best-selling book in the world for years!

There is no way on earth to explain it. Which perhaps is the only explanation. The answer? The Bible's durability is not found on earth; it is found in heaven. For the millions who have tested its claims and claimed its promises, there is but one answer: the Bible is God's book and God's voice.

As you read it, you would be wise to give some thought to two questions. What is the purpose of the Bible? and How do I study the Bible? Time spent reflecting on these two issues will greatly enhance your Bible study.

What is the purpose of the Bible?

Let the Bible itself answer that question.

Since you were a child you have known the Holy Scriptures which are able to make you wise. And that wisdom leads to salvation through faith in Christ Jesus. (2 Tim. 3:15 NCV)

The purpose of the Bible? Salvation. God's highest passion is to get his children home. His book, the Bible, describes his plan of salvation. The purpose of the Bible is to proclaim God's plan and passion to save his children.

That is the reason this book has endured through the centuries. It dares to tackle the toughest questions about life: Where do I go after I die? Is there a God? What do I do with my fears? The Bible offers answers to these crucial questions. It is the treasure map that leads us to God's highest treasure—eternal life.

LIFE Lessons

WITH MAX LUCADO

CONTENTS

But how do we use the Bible? Countless copies of Scripture sit unread on bookshelves and nightstands simply because people don't know how to read it. What can we do to make the Bible real in our lives?

The clearest answer is found in the words of Jesus. He promised:

Ask, and God will give to you. Search, and you will find. Knock, and the door will open for you. (Matt. 7:7 NCV)

The first step in understanding the Bible is asking God to help us. We should read prayerfully. If anyone understands God's Word, it is because of God and not the reader.

But the Helper will teach you everything and will cause you to remember all that I told you. The Helper is the Holy Spirit whom the Father will send in my name. (John 14:26 NCV)

Before reading the Bible, pray. Invite God to speak to you. Don't go to Scripture looking for your idea; go searching for his.

Not only should we read the Bible prayerfully; we should read it carefully. *Search and you will find* is the pledge. The Bible is not a newspaper to be skimmed but rather a mine to be quarried.

Search for it like silver, and hunt for it like hidden treasure. Then you will understand respect for the LORD, and you will find that you know God. (Prov. 2:4–5 NCV)

Any worthy find requires effort. The Bible is no exception. To understand the Bible you don't have to be brilliant, but you must be willing to roll up your sleeves and search.

Be a worker who is not ashamed and who uses the true teaching in the right way. (2 Tim. 2:15 NCV)

Here's a practical point. Study the Bible a bit at a time. Hunger is not satisfied by eating twenty-one meals in one sitting once a week. The body needs a steady diet to remain strong. So does the soul. When God sent food to his people in the wilderness, he didn't provide loaves already made. Instead, he sent them manna in the shape of *"thin flakes like frost . . . on the desert ground"* (Ex 16:14 NCV).

God gave manna in limited portions. God sends spiritual food the same way. He opens the heavens with just enough nutrients for today's hunger. He provides *"a command here, a command there. A rule here, a rule there. A little lesson here, a little lesson there"* (Isa. 28:10 NCV).

Don't be discouraged if your reading reaps a small harvest. Some days a lesser portion is all that is needed. What is important is to search every day for that day's message. A steady diet of God's Word over a lifetime builds a healthy soul and mind.

A little girl returned from her first day at school. Her mom asked, "Did you learn anything?"

"Apparently not enough," the girl responded, "I have to go back tomorrow and the next day and the next . . ."

Such is the case with learning. And such is the case with Bible study. Understanding comes little by little over a lifetime.

There is a third step in understanding the Bible. After the asking and seeking comes the knocking. After you ask and search, then knock.

Knock, and the door will open for you. (Matt. 7:7 NCV)

To knock is to stand at God's door. To make yourself available. To climb the steps, cross the porch, stand at the doorway, and volunteer. Knocking goes beyond the realm of thinking and into the realm of acting.

To knock is to ask, What can I do? How can I obey? Where can I go?

It's one thing to know what to do. It's another to do it. But for those who do it, those who choose to obey, a special reward awaits them.

The truly happy are those who carefully study God's perfect law that makes people free, and they continue to study it. They do not forget what they heard, but they obey what God's teaching says. Those who do this will be made happy. (James 1:25 NCV)

What a promise. Happiness comes to those who do what they read! It's the same with medicine. If you only read the label but ignore the pills, it won't help. It's the same with food. If you only read the recipe but never cook, you won't be fed. And it's the same with the Bible. If you only read the words but never obey, you'll never know the joy God has promised.

Ask. Search. Knock. Simple, isn't it? Why don't you give it a try? If you do, you'll see why you are holding the most remarkable book in history.

But how do we use the Bible? Countless copies of Scripture sit unread on bookshelves and nightstands simply because people don't know how to read it. What can we do to make the Bible real in our lives?

The clearest answer is found in the words of Jesus. He promised:

Ask, and God will give to you. Search, and you will find. Knock, and the door will open for you. (Matt. 7:7 NCV)

The first step in understanding the Bible is asking God to help us. We should read prayerfully. If anyone understands God's Word, it is because of God and not the reader.

But the Helper will teach you everything and will cause you to remember all that I told you. The Helper is the Holy Spirit whom the Father will send in my name. (John 14:26 NCV)

Before reading the Bible, pray. Invite God to speak to you. Don't go to Scripture looking for your idea; go searching for his.

Not only should we read the Bible prayerfully; we should read it carefully. *Search and you will find* is the pledge. The Bible is not a newspaper to be skimmed but rather a mine to be quarried.

Search for it like silver, and hunt for it like hidden treasure. Then you will understand respect for the LORD, and you will find that you know God. (Prov. 2:4–5 NCV)

Any worthy find requires effort. The Bible is no exception. To understand the Bible you don't have to be brilliant, but you must be willing to roll up your sleeves and search.

Be a worker who is not ashamed and who uses the true teaching in the right way. (2 Tim. 2:15 NCV)

Here's a practical point. Study the Bible a bit at a time. Hunger is not satisfied by eating twenty-one meals in one sitting once a week. The body needs a steady diet to remain strong. So does the soul. When God sent food to his people in the wilderness, he didn't provide loaves already made. Instead, he sent them manna in the shape of *"thin flakes like frost . . . on the desert ground"* (Ex 16:14 NCV).

God gave manna in limited portions. God sends spiritual food the same way. He opens the heavens with just enough nutrients for today's hunger. He provides *"a command here, a command there. A rule here, a rule there. A little lesson here, a little lesson there"* (Isa. 28:10 NCV).

Don't be discouraged if your reading reaps a small harvest. Some days a lesser portion is all that is needed. What is important is to search every day for that day's message. A steady diet of God's Word over a lifetime builds a healthy soul and mind.

A little girl returned from her first day at school. Her mom asked, "Did you learn anything?"

"Apparently not enough," the girl responded, "I have to go back tomorrow and the next day and the next . . ."

Such is the case with learning. And such is the case with Bible study. Understanding comes little by little over a lifetime.

There is a third step in understanding the Bible. After the asking and seeking comes the knocking. After you ask and search, then knock.

Knock, and the door will open for you. (Matt. 7:7 NCV)

To knock is to stand at God's door. To make yourself available. To climb the steps, cross the porch, stand at the doorway, and volunteer. Knocking goes beyond the realm of thinking and into the realm of acting.

To knock is to ask, What can I do? How can I obey? Where can I go?

It's one thing to know what to do. It's another to do it. But for those who do it, those who choose to obey, a special reward awaits them.

The truly happy are those who carefully study God's perfect law that makes people free, and they continue to study it. They do not forget what they heard, but they obey what God's teaching says. Those who do this will be made happy. (James 1:25 NCV)

What a promise. Happiness comes to those who do what they read! It's the same with medicine. If you only read the label but ignore the pills, it won't help. It's the same with food. If you only read the recipe but never cook, you won't be fed. And it's the same with the Bible. If you only read the words but never obey, you'll never know the joy God has promised.

Ask. Search. Knock. Simple, isn't it? Why don't you give it a try? If you do, you'll see why you are holding the most remarkable book in history.

INTRODUCTION TO THE BOOK OF ACTS

They aren't the same men.

Oh, I know they look like it. They have the same names. The same faces. The same mannerisms. They look the same. But they aren't. On the surface they appear no different. Peter is still brazen. Nathanael is still reflective. Philip is still calculating.

They look the same. But they aren't. They aren't the same men you read about in the last four books. The fellows you got to know in the Gospels? These are the ones, but they're different.

You'll see it. As you read you'll see it. In their eyes. You hear it in their voices. You feel it in their passion. These men have changed.

As you read you'll wonder—are these the same guys? The ones who doubted in Galilee? The ones who argued in Capernaum? The ones who ran for their lives in Gethsemane? You'll wonder, "Are these the same men?"

The answer is no. They are different. They have stood face-to-face with God. They have sat at the feet of the resurrected King. They are different.

Within them dwells a fire not found on earth. Christ has taught them. The Father has forgiven them. The Spirit indwells them. They are not the same.

And because they are different, so is the world.

Read their adventures and be encouraged. Read their adventures and be listening. What God did for them, he longs to do for you.

LESSON ONE

JESUS
CHANGES
LIVES

MAX
LUCADO

REFLECTION

Community. Unselfish sharing. Unity. These are things we hope to experience in our families, our churches, and our society. Unfortunately, these qualities are often lacking. The book of Acts, entitled the "Acts of the Apostles," records the continuation of the story of Jesus' disciples after Jesus ascended to heaven. The first followers of Jesus came from different backgrounds, yet demonstrated amazing community as the early church was formed. Think about your church. In what ways can you see the transforming power of Jesus' presence?

SITUATION

For almost two months Jerusalem had been buzzing with arguments, plots, a headline crucifixion, rumors of a resurrection, transformed lives, visits from the risen Jesus, and his sudden departure to heaven, witnessed by hundreds. Jesus' followers gathered to pray, and the Holy Spirit showed up! In the early-morning hours of Pentecost, a new sound was heard in the temple courts: Galileans were speaking various languages, praising God in tongues other than their own. A crowd gathered. Opinions and conclusions were reached. Then one of those disciples stood up and spoke. Peter, the transformed fisherman who had betrayed his Lord, delivered the first sermon, explaining from the Scriptures who Jesus really was and why he died. The results were remarkable.

OBSERVATION

Read Acts 2:36–47 from the NCV or the NKJV.

NCV

36 "So, all the people of Israel should know this truly: God has made Jesus—the man you nailed to the cross—both Lord and Christ." 37When the people heard this, they felt guilty and asked Peter and the other apostles, "What shall we do?"

38Peter said to them, "Change your hearts and lives and be baptized, each one of you, in the name of Jesus Christ for the forgiveness of your sins. And you will receive the gift of the Holy Spirit. 39This promise is for you, for your children, and for all who are far away. It is for everyone the Lord our God calls to himself."

40Peter warned them with many other words. He begged them, "Save yourselves from the evil of today's people!" 41Then those people who accepted what Peter said were baptized. About three thousand people were added to the number of believers that day. 42They spent their time learning the apostles' teaching, sharing, breaking bread, and praying together.

43The apostles were doing many miracles and signs, and everyone felt great respect for God. 44All the believers were together and shared everything. 45They would sell their land and the things they owned and then divide the money and give it to anyone who needed it. 46The believers met together in the Temple every day. They ate together in their homes, happy to share their food with joyful hearts. 47They praised God and were liked by all the people. Every day the Lord added those who were being saved to the group of believers.

NKJV

36 "Therefore let all the house of Israel know assuredly that God has made this Jesus, whom you crucified, both Lord and Christ." 37Now when they heard this, they were cut to the heart, and said to Peter and the rest of the apostles, "Men and brethren, what shall we do?"

38Then Peter said to them, "Repent, and let every one of you be baptized in the name of Jesus Christ for the remission of sins; and you shall receive the gift of the Holy Spirit. 39For the promise is to you and to your children, and to all who are afar off, as many as the Lord our God will call."

40And with many other words he testified and exhorted them, saying, "Be saved from this perverse generation." 41Then those who gladly received his word were baptized; and that day about three thousand souls were added to them. 42And they continued steadfastly in the apostles' doctrine and fellowship, in the breaking of bread, and in prayers. 43Then fear came upon every soul, and many wonders and signs were done through the apostles. 44Now all who believed were together, and had all things in common, 45and sold their possessions and goods, and divided them among all, as anyone had need.

46So continuing daily with one accord in the temple, and breaking bread from house to house, they ate their food with gladness and simplicity of heart, 47praising God and having favor with all the people. And the Lord added to the church daily those who were being saved.

EXPLORATION

1. What bold statement did Peter make to the crowd?

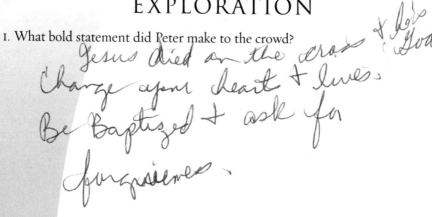

Jesus died on the cross & he's God
Change your heart & lives.
Be Baptized & ask for
forgiveness.

2. How did the people react to Peter's declaration?

They felt guilty & ask
Peter what to do.

3. What instructions did Peter give to the people?

Change your hearts
& lifes &
Be baptized
& ask for forgiveness

4. To whom is the Holy Spirit available?

Those who ask for forgiveness.

5. How did the new believers grow in their faith? How did they practice that faith with one another?

They felt great respect for God. They met in the temple every day — They shared their worldly gifts

INSPIRATION

A transformed group stood beside a transformed Peter as he announced some weeks later: "So, all the people of Israel should know this truly: God has made Jesus—the man you nailed to the cross—both Lord and Christ."

No timidity in his words. No reluctance. About three thousand people believed his message.

The apostles sparked a movement. The people became followers of the death-conqueror. They couldn't hear enough or say enough about him . . . Christ was their model, their message. They preached "Jesus Christ and him crucified," not for the lack of another topic, but because they couldn't exhaust this one.

What unlocked the doors of the apostles' hearts?

Simple. They saw Jesus. They encountered the Christ. Their sins collided with their Savior and their Savior won!

A lot of things would happen to them over the next few decades. Many nights would be spent away from home. Hunger would gnaw at their bellies. Rain would soak their skin. Stones would bruise their bodies. Shipwrecks, lashings, martyrdom. But there was a scene in the repertoire of memories that caused them to never look back: the betrayed coming back to find his betrayers; not to scourge them, but to send them. Not to criticize them for forgetting, but to commission them to remember. *Remember* that he who was dead is alive and they who were guilty have been forgiven. (From *Six Hours One Friday* by Max Lucado)

REACTION

6. What changes has Jesus made in your life?

7. What circumstances caused you to open your heart to God?

8. Why do some people resist the convicting work of the Holy Spirit?

9. The Holy Spirit gave Peter boldness to speak the truth. What ability or gift have you received from God?

10. How have you discovered the spiritual gifts God has given you?

11. How can you use your gifts to help bring others into God's kingdom?

LIFE LESSONS

Authentic followers of Jesus always have company. In fact, if we feel all alone in our faith, one of the explanations may be that we're not following Jesus as closely as we think we are. The first disciples went from feeling all alone to speaking out and discovering over three thousand new companions. The practice of faith involves others. Make it a point to pursue healthy relationships with other believers. Ask Jesus to change you into an agent of peace in every situation you find yourself in. Ask him to make you into good company.

DEVOTION

Father, we invite the powerful indwelling of your Spirit because we do not have the power to change ourselves. May we be open to your convicting work; may we be sincere; may we be willing to grow. Father, transform us into your likeness.

For more Bible passages about God's power to change people, see 1 Samuel 10:6; Romans 1:16–17; 8:9–14; 16:17–19; 2 Corinthians 3:18; Galatians 5:22; Ephesians 3:16–20; Colossians 1:10–12; 28–29; 2 Peter 1:3.

To complete the book of Acts during this twelve-part study, read Acts 1:1–2:47.

JOURNALING

In what area of my life have I resisted the Spirit's work? How can I change that attitude?

LESSON TWO

WE ARE
WITNESSES

MAX
LUCADO

REFLECTION

Think back to your life before you knew about Christ. Perhaps you were acutely aware that something was wrong with life. You were missing something. Or you may have had a vague and occasional feeling of unease. Then someone spoke words of truth into your life. Someone witnessed to you about what Jesus meant to him or her. Someone explained who Jesus was. Who helped you understand the truth of the gospel? How did they accomplish that task?

SITUATION

Days of excitement and new faith made the apostles' lives hectic and full. They had to stay focused. There were great spiritual and other needs everywhere. One day Peter and John had an eye-opening encounter with a crippled man. He was merely hoping for some financial help; the apostles gave him something far better.

OBSERVATION

Read Acts 3:1–16 from the NCV or the NKJV.

NCV

¹One day Peter and John went to the Temple at three o'clock, the time set each day for the afternoon prayer service. ²There, at the Temple gate called Beautiful Gate, was a man who had been crippled all his life. Every day he was carried to this gate to beg for money from the people going into the Temple. ³The man saw Peter and John going into the Temple and asked them for money. ⁴Peter and John looked straight at him and said, "Look at us!" ⁵The man looked at them, thinking they were going to give him some money. ⁶But Peter said, "I don't have any silver or gold, but I do have something else I can give you. By the power of Jesus Christ from Nazareth, stand up and walk!" ⁷Then Peter took the man's right hand and lifted him up. Immediately the man's feet and ankles became strong. ⁸He jumped up, stood on his feet, and began to walk. He went into the Temple with them, walking and jumping and praising God. ⁹⁻¹⁰All the people recognized him as the crippled man who always sat by the Beautiful Gate begging for money. Now they saw this same man walking and praising God, and they were amazed. They wondered how this could happen.

¹¹While the man was holding on to Peter and John, all the people were amazed and ran to them at Solomon's Porch. ¹²When Peter saw this, he said to them, "People of Israel, why are you surprised? You are looking at us as if it were our own power or goodness that made this man walk. ¹³The God of Abraham, Isaac, and Jacob, the God of our ancestors, gave glory to Jesus, his servant. But you handed him over to be killed. Pilate decided to let him go free, but you told Pilate you did not want Jesus. ¹⁴You did not want the One who is holy and good but asked Pilate to give you a murderer instead. ¹⁵And so you killed the One who gives life, but God raised him from the dead. We are witnesses to this. ¹⁶It was faith in Jesus that made this crippled man well. You can see this man, and you know him. He was made completely well because of trust in Jesus, and you all saw it happen!

NKJV

¹Now Peter and John went up together to the temple at the hour of prayer, the ninth hour. ²And a certain man lame from his mother's womb was carried, whom they laid daily at the gate of the temple which is called Beautiful, to ask alms from those who entered the temple; ³who, seeing Peter and John about to go into the temple, asked for alms. ⁴And fixing his eyes on him, with John, Peter said, "Look at us." ⁵So he gave them his attention, expecting to receive something from them. ⁶Then Peter said, "Silver and gold I do not have, but what I do have I give you: In the name of Jesus Christ of Nazareth, rise up and walk." ⁷And he took him by the right hand and lifted him up, and immediately his feet and ankle bones received strength. ⁸So he, leaping up, stood and walked and entered the temple with them—walking, leaping, and praising God. ⁹And all the people saw him walking and praising God. ¹⁰Then they knew that it was he who sat begging alms at the Beautiful Gate of the temple; and they were filled with wonder and amazement at what had happened to him.

11Now as the lame man who was healed held on to Peter and John, all the people ran together to them in the porch which is called Solomon's, greatly amazed. 12So when Peter saw it, he responded to the people: "Men of Israel, why do you marvel at this? Or why look so intently at us, as though by our own power or godliness we had made this man walk? 13The God of Abraham, Isaac, and Jacob, the God of our fathers, glorified His Servant Jesus, whom you delivered up and denied in the presence of Pilate, when he was determined to let Him go. 14But you denied the Holy One and the Just, and asked for a murderer to be granted to you, 15and killed the Prince of life, whom God raised from the dead, of which we are witnesses. 16And His name, through faith in His name, has made this man strong, whom you see and know. Yes, the faith which comes through Him has given him this perfect soundness in the presence of you all."

EXPLORATION

1. What were Peter and John unable to give the crippled man? What did they give?

2. How did the crippled man react to the miracle?

3. How did the people at the temple respond to Peter and John after they heard about the miracle?

4. What opportunity did this miracle provide for Peter?

5. How did Peter explain the healing of the crippled man?

INSPIRATION

There's a story about a lady who had a small house on the seashore of Ireland at the turn of the century. She was quite wealthy but also quite frugal. The people were surprised, then, when she decided to be among the first to have electricity in her home.

Several weeks after the installation, a meter reader appeared at her door. He asked if her electricity was working well, and she assured him it was. "I'm wondering if you can explain something to me," he said. "Your meter shows scarcely any usage. Are you using your power?"

"Certainly," she answered. "Each evening when the sun sets, I turn on my lights just long enough to light my candles; then I turn them off."

She's tapped into the power but doesn't use it. Her house is connected but not altered. Don't we make the same mistake? We, too—with our souls saved but our hearts unchanged—are connected but not altered. Trusting Christ for salvation but resisting transformation. We occasionally flip the switch, but most of the time we settle for shadows.

What would happen if we left the light on? What would happen if we not only flipped the switch but lived in the light? What changes would occur if we set about the task of dwelling in the radiance of Christ?

No doubt about it: God has ambitious plans for us. The same one who saved your soul longs to remake your heart. His plan is nothing short of a total transformation: "He decided from the outset to shape the lives of those who love him along the same lines as the life of his Son" (Rom. 8:29 MSG). (From *Just Like Jesus* by Max Lucado)

REACTION

6. What can we learn from Peter's example about spreading the gospel?

7. Why is it important for us to encourage others to follow Jesus?

8. What does it mean to be bold witnesses for Christ?

9. What excuses do Christians use to keep quiet about their faith?

10. What steps can you take to prepare yourself to explain the gospel to others?

11. Think of one person who does not know Christ. When can you share the gospel with that person?

LIFE LESSONS

Witnessing is simply sharing what you have seen. Start each day with a heartfelt request: "Lord, send someone my way today whose need is so obvious that even I can't miss it! Remind me that what I have in you is the very best gift I could give that person, no matter what he or she has asked of me. And when I meet that person, help me resist the temptation to come up with something witty to say but to, instead, simply depend on you for what to say."

DEVOTION

Father, you give us many opportunities to proclaim your salvation message, yet we often shirk back from those opportunities in fearful silence. Forgive us, Father. Fill us with courage to boldly speak the truth in love. Teach us what it means to be your witnesses.

For more Bible passages about witnessing, see Mark 5:19; 16:15; Acts 1:8; 2 Corinthians 4:13–14; Colossians 4:5–6; 2 Timothy 4:2; 1 Peter 3:15–16.

To complete the book of Acts during this twelve-part study, read Acts 3:1–4:37.

JOURNALING

How have I used the opportunities God has given me to share the gospel?

TRIED AND TESTED

MAX
LUCADO

REFLECTION

Jesus said that his followers would experience tough times. "If they hated me, they'll hate you too," he said. Being bold and "out there" about your faith is not easy. And it wasn't easy for the early Christians either. Their boldness landed them in some pretty hot water. Think of someone you know who has suffered hardship, opposition, or worse because of his or her faith. What do you admire about that person?

SITUATION

In the aftermath of Jesus' resurrection, the message about forgiveness and new life seemed unstoppable. Boldness bred popularity. It also provoked a jealous backlash. The religious establishment in Jerusalem felt threatened by these brash Jesus-followers. They decided to try intimidation as a tactic to silence those most prominent in spreading the news about Jesus.

OBSERVATION

Read Acts 5:17–33 from the NCV or the NKJV.

NCV

17The high priest and all his friends (a group called the Sadducees) became very jealous. 18They took the apostles and put them in jail. 19But during the night, an angel of the Lord opened the doors of the jail and led the apostles outside. The angel said, 20"Go stand in the Temple and tell the people everything about this new life." 21When the apostles heard this, they obeyed and went into the Temple early in the morning and continued teaching.

When the high priest and his friends arrived, they called a meeting of the Jewish leaders and all the important older Jewish men. They sent some men to the jail to bring the apostles to them. 22But, upon arriving, the officers could not find the apostles. So they went back and reported to the Jewish leaders. 23They said, "The jail was closed and locked, and the guards were standing at the doors. But when we opened the doors, the jail was empty!" 24Hearing this, the captain of the Temple guards and the leading priests were confused and wondered what was happening.

25Then someone came and told them, "Listen! The men you put in jail are standing in the Temple teaching the people." 26Then the captain and his men went out and brought the apostles back. But the soldiers did not use force, because they were afraid the people would stone them to death.

27The soldiers brought the apostles to the meeting and made them stand before the Jewish leaders. The high priest questioned them, 28saying, "We gave you strict orders not to continue teaching in that name. But look, you have filled Jerusalem with your teaching and are trying to make us responsible for this man's death."

29Peter and the other apostles answered, "We must obey God, not human authority! 30You killed Jesus by hanging him on a cross. But God, the God of our ancestors, raised Jesus up from the dead! 31Jesus is the One whom God raised to be on his right side, as Leader and Savior. Through him, all Jewish people could change their hearts and lives and have their sins forgiven. 32We saw all these things happen. The Holy Spirit, whom God has given to all who obey him, also proves these things are true."

33When the Jewish leaders heard this, they became angry and wanted to kill them.

NKJV

17Then the high priest rose up, and all those who were with him (which is the sect of the Sadducees), and they were filled with indignation, 18and laid their hands on the apostles and put them in the common prison. 19But at night an angel of the Lord opened the prison doors and brought them out, and said, 20 "Go, stand in the temple and speak to the people all the words of this life."

21And when they heard that, they entered the temple early in the morning and taught. But the high priest and those with him came and called the council together, with all the elders of the children of Israel, and sent to the prison to have them brought.

22But when the officers came and did not find them in the prison, they returned and reported, 23saying, "Indeed we found the prison shut securely, and the guards standing outside before the doors; but when we opened them, we found no one inside!" 24Now when the high priest, the captain of the temple, and the chief priests heard these things, they wondered what the outcome would be. 25So one came and told them, saying, "Look, the men whom you put in prison are standing in the temple and teaching the people!"

26Then the captain went with the officers and brought them without violence, for they feared the people, lest they should be stoned. 27And when they had brought them, they set them before the council. And the high priest asked them, 28saying, "Did we not strictly command you not to teach in this name? And look, you have filled Jerusalem with your doctrine, and intend to bring this Man's blood on us!"

29But Peter and the other apostles answered and said: "We ought to obey God rather than men. 30The God of our fathers raised up Jesus whom you murdered by hanging on a tree. 31Him God has exalted to His right hand to be Prince and Savior, to give repentance to Israel and forgiveness of sins. 32And we are His witnesses to these things, and so also is the Holy Spirit whom God has given to those who obey Him." 33When they heard this, they were furious and plotted to kill them.

EXPLORATION

1. What was the problem between the apostles and the religious leaders?

2. How did the high priest try to stop the disciples from preaching?

3. How were the disciples able to continue their ministry?

4. What accusations did the high priest make against Peter and the other apostles?

5. How did the apostles deal with the opposition of the religious leaders?

INSPIRATION

On God's anvil. Perhaps you've been there.

Melted down. Formless. Undone.

I know. I've been on it. It's rough. It's a spiritual slump, a famine. The fire goes out. Although the fire may flame for a moment, it soon disappears. We drift downward. Downward into the foggy valley of question, the misty lowland of discouragement. Motivation wanes. Desire is distant. Responsibilities are depressing.

Passion? It slips out the door.

Enthusiasm? Are you kidding?

Anvil time.

It can be caused by a death, a breakup, going broke, going prayerless. The light switch is flipped off and the room darkens . . .

On the anvil.

Brought face to face with God out of the utter realization that we have nowhere else to go. Jesus, in the Garden. Peter, with a tear-streamed face. David, after Bathsheba. Elijah and the "still, small voice." Paul, blind in Damascus.

Pound, pound, pound.

I hope you're not on the anvil. (Unless you need to be and, if so, I hope you are.) Anvil time is not to be avoided; it's to be experienced. Although the tunnel is dark, it does go through the mountain. Anvil time reminds us of who we are and who God is. We shouldn't try to escape it. To escape it could be to escape God.

God sees our life from beginning to end. He may lead us through a storm at age thirty so we can endure a hurricane at age sixty. An instrument is useful only if it's in the right shape. A dull ax or a bent screwdriver needs attention, and so do we. A good blacksmith keeps his tools in shape. So does God.

Should God place you on his anvil, be thankful. It means he thinks you're still worth reshaping. (From *Shaped by God* by Max Lucado)

REACTION

6. What do people usually do when life gets difficult?

7. What lessons can be learned from experiencing pain?

8. What good has come from a difficult experience in your life?

9. What opposition do believers face today?

10. What can we learn from the apostles' example about coping with criticism and unfair treatment?

11. How can we develop a joyful spirit?

LIFE LESSONS

We like the idea of being used by God, but often dislike the measures God takes to prepare us for service. We like the idea of doing God's work, but dislike the reality of how much God's work will cost us. Jesus told us to count the cost (see Luke 14:25–33). We like the pleasure of knowing God; we dislike the pressure that comes from knowing God. Jesus compared the experience of following him to the task of carrying a cross. Gotten many slivers lately? If so, don't lose hope. Nothing is ever wasted, and God will never leave you.

DEVOTION

Father, we believe that when we meet you face-to-face, any trials that we endured on this earth will seem small. Help us remember that any earthly struggle is small in comparison to the great God we serve.

For more Bible passages about trials and testing, see Genesis 22:1; Job 23:10; Psalm 66:10; Isaiah 48:10; 2 Corinthians 4:8–9, 16–18; 2 Thessalonians 1:4–7; Hebrews 10:32–34; James 1:2–4, 12; 5:10–11; 1 Peter 2:20–21; 4:12–19; 5:10.

To complete the book of Acts during this twelve-part study, read Acts 5:1–42.

JOURNALING

How do I need to change my attitudes toward problems and difficulties in my life?

GETTING ALONG WITH OTHERS

MAX LUCADO

REFLECTION

From an early age most of us were taught about how to get along with others. If we were blessed with siblings, one of the first words we learned to say was "mine," and one of the first things our parents tried to teach us was "share." But sharing and serving don't come naturally. Most of us are pretty self-centered. What is the best advice you've heard about getting along with people? How have you put it into practice?

SITUATION

Even the best plan has flaws. Human responses, even the best intentioned, still leave some needs unmet. As the community of followers of Jesus expanded, certain challenges naturally developed. They may have revealed unforeseen racial and social issues. But the presenting problem had to do with one group's basic needs and someone being willing to serve. The apostles were asked to solve this practical problem. Note how they gave the responsibility back to the people.

OBSERVATION

Read Acts 6:1–15 from the NCV or the NKJV.

NCV

¹The number of followers was growing. But during this same time, the Greek-speaking followers had an argument with the other Jewish followers. The Greek-speaking widows were not getting their share of the food that was given out every day. ²The twelve apostles called the whole group of followers together and said, "It is not right for us to stop our work of teaching God's word in order to serve tables. ³So, brothers and sisters, choose seven of your own men who are good, full of the Spirit and full of wisdom. We will put them in charge of this work. ⁴Then we can continue to pray and to teach the word of God."

⁵The whole group liked the idea, so they chose these seven men: Stephen (a man with great faith and full of the Holy Spirit), Philip, Procorus, Nicanor, Timon, Parmenas, and Nicolas (a man from Antioch who had become a Jew). ⁶Then they put these men before the apostles, who prayed and laid their hands on them.

⁷The word of God was continuing to spread. The group of followers in Jerusalem increased, and a great number of the Jewish priests believed and obeyed.

⁸Stephen was richly blessed by God who gave him the power to do great miracles and signs among the people. ⁹But some Jewish people were against him. They belonged to the synagogue of Free Men (as it was called), which included Jewish people from Cyrene, Alexandria, Cilicia, and Asia. They all came and argued with Stephen.

¹⁰But the Spirit was helping him to speak with wisdom, and his words were so strong that they could not argue with him. ¹¹So they secretly urged some men to say, "We heard Stephen speak against Moses and against God."

¹²This upset the people, the older Jewish leaders, and the teachers of the law. They came and grabbed Stephen and brought him to a meeting of the Jewish leaders. ¹³They brought in some people to tell lies about Stephen, saying, "This man is always speaking against this holy place and the law of Moses. ¹⁴We heard him say that Jesus from Nazareth will destroy this place and that Jesus will change the customs Moses gave us." ¹⁵All the people in the meeting were watching Stephen closely and saw that his face looked like the face of an angel.

NKJV

Now in those days, when the number of the disciples was multiplying, there arose a complaint against the Hebrews by the Hellenists, because their widows were neglected in the daily distribution. ²Then the twelve summoned the multitude of the disciples and said, "It is not desirable that we should leave the word of God and serve tables. ³Therefore, brethren, seek out from among you seven men of good reputation, full of the Holy Spirit and wisdom, whom we may appoint over this business; ⁴but we will give ourselves continually to prayer and to the ministry of the word."

⁵*And the saying pleased the whole multitude. And they chose Stephen, a man full of faith and the Holy Spirit, and Philip, Prochorus, Nicanor, Timon, Parmenas, and Nicolas, a proselyte from Antioch,* ⁶*whom they set before the apostles; and when they had prayed, they laid hands on them.*

⁷*Then the word of God spread, and the number of the disciples multiplied greatly in Jerusalem, and a great many of the priests were obedient to the faith.*

⁸*And Stephen, full of faith and power, did great wonders and signs among the people.* ⁹*Then there arose some from what is called the Synagogue of the Freedmen (Cyrenians, Alexandrians, and those from Cilicia and Asia), disputing with Stephen.* ¹⁰*And they were not able to resist the wisdom and the Spirit by which he spoke.* ¹¹*Then they secretly induced men to say, "We have heard him speak blasphemous words against Moses and God."* ¹²*And they stirred up the people, the elders, and the scribes; and they came upon him, seized him, and brought him to the council.* ¹³*They also set up false witnesses who said, "This man does not cease to speak blasphemous words against this holy place and the law;* ¹⁴*for we have heard him say that this Jesus of Nazareth will destroy this place and change the customs which Moses delivered to us."* ¹⁵*And all who sat in the council, looking steadfastly at him, saw his face as the face of an angel.*

EXPLORATION

1. What problem does this passage describe that arose in the early church regarding people's needs?

The greek widows not getting enough food.

2. What solution did the apostles offer? Why didn't they volunteer to be the solution?

for the followers to choose 7 men + women to come up with a solution — The apostles were busy praying + teaching God's word.

3. How did the group respond to the apostles' idea?

They liked the idea

4. What does this passage reveal about Stephen's character and relationship with God?

He was blessed by God + was given power to do miracles.

5. How did God use Stephen to help the early church?

God gave him wisdom to spread his word

INSPIRATION

What would happen if we accepted our place as Son reflectors?

Such a shift comes so stubbornly, however. We've been demanding our way and stamping our feet since infancy. Aren't we all born with a default drive set on selfishness? *I want a spouse who makes me happy and coworkers who always ask my opinion. I want weather that suits me and traffic that helps me and a government that serves me. It is all about me.* We relate to the advertisement that headlined, "For the man who thinks the world revolves around him." A prominent actress justified her appearance in a porn magazine by saying, "I wanted to express myself."

Self-promotion. Self-preservation. Self-centeredness. It's all about me!

They all told us it was, didn't they? Weren't we urged to look out for number one? Find our place in the sun? Make a name for ourselves? We thought self-celebration would make us happy . . .

But what chaos this philosophy creates. What if a symphony orchestra followed such an approach? Can you imagine an orchestra with an "It's all about me" outlook? Each artist clamoring for self-expression. Tubas blasting nonstop. Percussionists pounding to get attention. The cellist shoving the flutist out of the center stage chair. The trumpeter standing atop the conductor's stool tooting his horn. Sheet music disregarded. Conductor ignored. What do you have but an endless tune-up session!

Harmony? Hardly.

Happiness? Are the musicians happy to be in the group? Not at all. Who enjoys contributing to a cacophony?

36

You don't. We don't. We were not made to live this way. But aren't we guilty of doing just that?

No wonder our homes are so noisy, businesses so stress-filled, government so cutthroat, and harmony so rare. If you think it's all about you, and I think it's all about me, we have no hope for a melody. We've chased so many skinny rabbits that we've missed the fat one: the God-centered life.

What would happen if we took our places and played our parts? If we played the music the Maestro gave us to play? If we made his song our highest priority?

Would we see a change in families? We'd certainly *hear* a change. Less "Here is what I want!" More "What do you suppose God wants?" (From *It's Not About Me* by Max Lucado)

REACTION

6. What causes tension and disagreements in the church today?

7. Why is it important for Christians to get along?

8. What can we learn from the early church leaders about resolving our differences?

9. What happens when believers criticize and argue with one another?

10. What character traits do believers need to get along with one another?

11. How can we cultivate these qualities?

LIFE LESSONS

Life isn't measured by how many problems we have but by how we respond to them. That's what we can learn from the apostles as they formed the first church. They were starting a brand new thing; there was no model for them to follow. Challenges and disagreements were bound to happen. They chose to work together to overcome the problems. We can too. When Jesus informed us that we would have trouble (John 16:33), he did not give us permission to be overcome by trouble, but to accept his help to overcome it!

DEVOTION

Father, we pray that your church would be unified in love and purpose. Teach us how to sow seeds of peace and harmony. Help us to overcome trouble, not by blaming others, but by counting on you! Help us to resolve our differences lovingly, so that unbelievers would be drawn into your family because of the love we share. Teach us to think more in terms of "It's not about me."

For more Bible passages about getting along with people, see Proverbs 17:14; Romans 12:16; 15:5–7; 1 Corinthians 1:10; 3:3; 6:1–7; Ephesians 4:2–4; Philippians 2:3–4; 1 Thessalonians 5:12–15; Hebrews 2:14–18; 1 Peter 3:8–9.

To complete the book of Acts during this twelve-part study, read Acts 6:1–15.

JOURNALING

What do I usually do when I feel tension in a relationship? How can I improve the way I resolve conflicts?

LOOKING
TO JESUS

MAX
LUCADO

REFLECTION

As Christians, our aim is to live and die for God's glory. By looking to Jesus for grace and mercy, we can face the tough times of life. The passage today describes a scene in which an early follower of Jesus faces death and glorifies God in a very difficult situation. Think about someone that you know who has faced a life-threatening situation with faith and courage. How did he or she do it?

Mother in law

SITUATION

Stephen didn't have the reputation that surrounded the original disciples. The religious establishment feared the popularity of the apostles, but they decided Stephen was expendable. So when he began to teach, they put him on trial. False witnesses were hired to create a case. Stephen made an impassioned statement, not so much in his own defense but in order to urge his opponents to give Jesus serious consideration. As he neared the end of his remarks and his life, Stephen made some lasting statements worth pondering.

OBSERVATION

Read Acts 7:51–60 from the NCV or the NKJV.

NCV

⁵¹Stephen continued speaking: "You stubborn people! You have not given your hearts to God, nor will you listen to him! You are always against what the Holy Spirit is trying to tell you, just as your ancestors were. ⁵²Your ancestors tried to hurt every prophet who ever lived. Those prophets said long ago that the One who is good would come, but your ancestors killed them. And now you have turned against and killed the One who is good. ⁵³You received the law of Moses, which God gave you through his angels, but you haven't obeyed it."

⁵⁴When the leaders heard this, they became furious. They were so mad they were grinding their teeth at Stephen. ⁵⁵But Stephen was full of the Holy Spirit. He looked up to heaven and saw the glory of God and Jesus standing at God's right side. ⁵⁶He said, "Look! I see heaven open and the Son of Man standing at God's right side."

⁵⁷Then they shouted loudly and covered their ears and all ran at Stephen. ⁵⁸They took him out of the city and began to throw stones at him to kill him. And those who told lies against Stephen left their coats with a young man named Saul. ⁵⁹While they were throwing stones, Stephen prayed, "Lord Jesus, receive my spirit." ⁶⁰He fell on his knees and cried in a loud voice, "Lord, do not hold this sin against them." After Stephen said this, he died.

NKJV

⁵¹ "You stiff-necked and uncircumcised in heart and ears! You always resist the Holy Spirit; as your fathers did, so do you. ⁵²Which of the prophets did your fathers not persecute? And they killed those who foretold the coming of the Just One, of whom you now have become the betrayers and murderers, ⁵³who have received the law by the direction of angels and have not kept it."

⁵⁴When they heard these things they were cut to the heart, and they gnashed at him with their teeth. ⁵⁵But he, being full of the Holy Spirit, gazed into heaven and saw the glory of God, and Jesus standing at the right hand of God, ⁵⁶and said, "Look! I see the heavens opened and the Son of Man standing at the right hand of God!"

⁵⁷Then they cried out with a loud voice, stopped their ears, and ran at him with one accord; ⁵⁸and they cast him out of the city and stoned him. And the witnesses laid down their clothes at the feet of a young man named Saul. ⁵⁹And they stoned Stephen as he was calling on God and saying, "Lord Jesus, receive my spirit." ⁶⁰Then he knelt down and cried out with a loud voice, "Lord, do not charge them with this sin." And when he had said this, he fell asleep.

EXPLORATION

1. What accusations did Stephen make against the members of the ruling council? *They were stubborn & they killed the one who is good.*

2. To whom did Stephen compare the religious leaders? Why? *Their ancestors*

3. Why did Stephen's speech infuriate his adversaries? *Because he said they hadn't obeyed the law of moses which God gave them.*

4. How did Stephen face his impending death? To whom did he look?

He prayed to Jesus to recieve his soul —

5. What do Stephen's last words reveal about his character?

He knew how to forgive his enemies. Faithful

INSPIRATION

The story of young Matthew Huffman came across my desk the week I was writing this chapter. He was the six-year-old son of missionaries in Salvador, Brazil. One morning he began to complain of fever. As his temperature went up, he began losing his eyesight. His mother and father put him in the car and raced him to the hospital.

As they were driving and he was lying on his mother's lap, he did something his parents will never forget. He extended his hand in the air. His mother took it and he pulled it away. He extended it again. She again took it and he, again, pulled it back and reached into the air. Confused, the mother asked her son, "What are you reaching for, Matthew?"

"I'm reaching for Jesus' hand," he answered. And with those words he closed his eyes and slid into a coma from which he never would awaken. He died two days later, a victim of bacterial meningitis.

Of all the things he didn't learn in his short life, he'd learned the most important: who to reach for in the hour of death. (From *And the Angels Were Silent* by Max Lucado)

REACTION

6. Why do you think Stephen was able to face death courageously?

He's parents had taught him well. He was able to understand what & how important Christ is. He looked toward God

7. How does Stephen's example encourage you?

I need to face the reality
of any situation even if
it doesn't turn out the
way I want. Look to God
Call on the holy spirit.

8. Why do you suppose we look to ourselves for strength rather than depending on God?

Because we want to
be in control.

9. Where do you usually turn for help when you are in trouble?

It varies —

10. What happens when we depend on ourselves or others to carry us through painful experiences?

tb. Eventually we need to turn to God

II. Think of an instance when you received God's help during a difficult time. What happened?

LIFE LESSONS

When the crisis moments come, when death looms, when dreams and plans suddenly disappear, to whom do we turn? Almost every day provides us with small and large opportunities to trust, to reach for Jesus' hand. We are most likely to reach for him in our final moments before death if we've been in the habit of doing that all our lives.

DEVOTION

Father, put your hands and your arms around us and embrace us. Carry us through the valleys, giving us strength for today and courage for tomorrow. Teach us to reach out and seek you in all things.

For more Bible passages about turning to God, see Psalms 34:5; 105:4; 142:5–6; Acts 3:19; Hebrews 3:1; 12:2; 1 Peter 5:9.

To complete the book of Acts during this twelve-part study, read Acts 7:1–60.

JOURNALING

In what area of my life do I need Jesus' help? How can I show my dependence on him?

THE HOLY SPIRIT'S LEADING

MAX LUCADO

REFLECTION

Some of life's best experiences begin unexpectedly. There was a time when our best friend was still a stranger. Did we plan to meet? Probably not. Great opportunities to help someone or to work together on a project might be waiting just around the bend, closer than tomorrow. God knows about these moments before they happen. Would they happen more often if we listened carefully to what he says to us? Think of a time when you felt compelled to help someone. What did you do to help that person? How would you describe that moment as a divine encounter that God arranged?

SITUATION

Two men named Philip appear in the accounts of the early church. One was an apostle; the other was chosen along with Stephen as one of the deacons. Like Stephen, Philip had a way with people. He was also sensitive to God's leading. So it was that he found himself walking along a major road leading south from Jerusalem, through Gaza, toward Egypt and Ethiopia. Soon he heard the sounds of a traveling caravan behind him. He would soon discover that God had arranged an appointment for him.

OBSERVATION

Read Acts 8:26–40 from the NCV or the NKJV.

NCV

²⁶An angel of the Lord said to Philip, "Get ready and go south to the road that leads down to Gaza from Jerusalem—the desert road." ²⁷So Philip got ready and went. On the road he saw a man from Ethiopia, a eunuch. He was an important officer in the service of Candace, the queen of the Ethiopians; he was responsible for taking care of all her money. He had gone to Jerusalem to worship. ²⁸Now, as he was on his way home, he was sitting in his chariot reading from the Book of Isaiah, the prophet. ²⁹The Spirit said to Philip, "Go to that chariot and stay near it."

³⁰So when Philip ran toward the chariot, he heard the man reading from Isaiah the prophet. Philip asked, "Do you understand what you are reading?"

³¹He answered, "How can I understand unless someone explains it to me?" Then he invited Philip to climb in and sit with him. ³²The portion of Scripture he was reading was this:

"He was like a sheep being led to be killed.

He was quiet, as a lamb is quiet while its wool is being cut;

he never opened his mouth.

³³He was shamed and was treated unfairly.

He died without children to continue his family.

His life on earth has ended."

³⁴The officer said to Philip, "Please tell me, who is the prophet talking about—himself or someone else?" ³⁵Philip began to speak, and starting with this same Scripture, he told the man the Good News about Jesus. ³⁶While they were traveling down the road, they came to some water. The officer said, "Look, here is water. What is stopping me from being baptized?" ³⁸Then the officer commanded the chariot to stop. Both Philip and the officer went down into the water, and Philip baptized him. ³⁹When they came up out of the water, the Spirit of the Lord took Philip away; the officer never saw him again. And the officer continued on his way home, full of joy. ⁴⁰But Philip appeared in a city called Azotus and preached the Good News in all the towns on the way from Azotus to Caesarea.

NKJV

²⁶Now an angel of the Lord spoke to Philip, saying, "Arise and go toward the south along the road which goes down from Jerusalem to Gaza." This is desert. ²⁷So he arose and went. And behold, a man of Ethiopia, a eunuch of great authority under Candace the queen of the Ethiopians, who had charge of all her treasury, and had come to Jerusalem to worship, ²⁸was returning. And sitting in his chariot, he was reading Isaiah the prophet. ²⁹Then the Spirit said to Philip, "Go near and overtake this chariot."

³⁰So Philip ran to him, and heard him reading the prophet Isaiah, and said, "Do you understand what you are reading?"

³¹And he said, "How can I, unless someone guides me?" And he asked Philip to come up and sit with him. ³²The place in the Scripture which he read was this:

"He was led as a sheep to the slaughter;

And as a lamb before its shearer is silent,

So He opened not His mouth.

³³ In His humiliation His justice was taken away,

And who will declare His generation?

For His life is taken from the earth."

³⁴So the eunuch answered Philip and said, "I ask you, of whom does the prophet say this, of himself or of some other man?" ³⁵Then Philip opened his mouth, and beginning at this Scripture, preached Jesus to him. ³⁶Now as they went down the road, they came to some water. And the eunuch said, "See, here is water. What hinders me from being baptized?"

³⁷Then Philip said, "If you believe with all your heart, you may."

And he answered and said, "I believe that Jesus Christ is the Son of God."

³⁸So he commanded the chariot to stand still. And both Philip and the eunuch went down into the water, and he baptized him. ³⁹Now when they came up out of the water, the Spirit of the Lord caught Philip away, so that the eunuch saw him no more; and he went on his way rejoicing. ⁴⁰But Philip was found at Azotus. And passing through, he preached in all the cities till he came to Caesarea.

EXPLORATION

1. What examples of the Holy Spirit's leading do you see in this story?

a spirit told philip to go near + overtake the chariot.

2. Why did God ask Philip to leave his preaching and go down a desert road?

To baptize the eunuch

3. What was significant about the person Philip encountered on the road?

He was not accepted by the Jews as being a whole person.

4. How did Philip handle the opportunity that God gave him?

He baptized the eunuch

5. What was the result of Philip's obedience to God?

The Eunuch became a christian.

INSPIRATION

You've heard the voice whispering your name, haven't you? You've felt the nudge to go and sensed the urge to speak. Hasn't it occurred to you?

You invite a couple over for coffee. Nothing heroic, just a nice evening with old friends. But from the moment you enter, you can feel the tension. Colder than glaciers, they are. You can tell something is wrong. Typically you're not one to inquire, but you feel a concern that won't be silent. So you ask.

You are in a business meeting where one of your co-workers gets raked over the coals. Everyone else is thinking, *I'm glad that wasn't me.* But the Holy Spirit is leading you to think, *How hard this must be.* So, after the meeting you approach the employee and express your concern.

You notice the fellow on the other side of the church auditorium. He looks a bit out of place, what with his strange clothing and all. You learn that he is from Africa, in town on business. The next Sunday he is back. And the third Sunday he is present. You introduce yourself. He tells you how he is fascinated by the faith and how he wants to learn more. Rather than offer to teach him, you simply urge him to read the Bible.

Later in the week, you regret not being more direct. You call the office where he is consulting and learn that he is leaving today for home. You know in your heart you can't let him leave. So you rush to the airport and find him awaiting his flight, with a Bible open on his lap.

"Do you understand what you are reading?" you inquire.

"How can I, unless someone explains it to me?"

And so you, like Philip, explain. And he, like the Ethiopian, believes. Baptism is requested and baptism is offered. He catches a later flight and you catch a glimpse of what it means to be led by the Spirit.

Were there lights? You just lit one. Were there voices? You just were one. Was there a miracle? You just witnessed one. Who knows? If the Bible were being written today, that might be your name in the eighth chapter of Acts. (From *When God Whispers Your Name* by Max Lucado)

REACTION

6. How does God's Spirit lead us?

7. Why is it important to be sensitive to the Holy Spirit?

8. How can we learn to recognize God's voice?

9. When have you felt the Holy Spirit nudging you? What did you do?

10. What holds us back from obeying God?

11. What is the potential danger in ignoring the Spirit's leading?

LIFE LESSONS

Is there anyone you are not willing to tell about Jesus? Is there any place you are not willing to take the good news? Ask God to give you the same kind of willingness, attentiveness, and courage that you see in Philip. Let him direct you where he wants you to go.

DEVOTION

Father, too many times we fail to hear you speaking to us. Remind us to be quiet before you so that we can hear your voice. May we make decisions based on your leading, not according to our goals and desires. But most of all, Father, help us to cherish the gift of your Spirit.

For more Bible passages about the Holy Spirit's leading, see Matthew 4:1; Luke 4:18; John 6:63; 14:26; 16:13; Acts 2:4; Romans 8:5, 26–27; Galatians 5:25; 2 Peter 1:21.

To complete the book of Acts during this twelve-part study, read Acts 8:1–40.

JOURNALING

What can I do to listen to the Spirit's guidance today? How ready am I to cooperate if God speaks into my life?

LESSON SEVEN

GOD'S
SAVING
POWER

MAX
LUCADO

REFLECTION

God is the great "interrupter." At times he seems to slowly sneak up in our lives; other times he abruptly intrudes into our plans. God chooses the approach, knowing well how to get our attention. No matter what road we may find ourselves on, God's power is always more than enough to turn us around. Think of a time you have seen God's power unexpectedly revealed in the life of a friend, or perhaps in your own life. What happened to that person? How was God's power evident?

SITUATION

After Stephen's death, a Pharisee named Saul went on a rampage of persecution against Christians. When the followers of Jesus left Jerusalem, Saul went after them. He heard there was a large group in Damascus, so he obtained permission to travel there with an armed company to capture believers and bring them back to Jerusalem for trial, imprisonment, and probably death. On the road to Damascus, Jesus ambushed Saul.

OBSERVATION

Read Acts 9:3–20 from the NCV or the NKJV.

NCV

³So Saul headed toward Damascus. As he came near the city, a bright light from heaven suddenly flashed around him. ⁴Saul fell to the ground and heard a voice saying to him, "Saul, Saul! Why are you persecuting me?"

⁵Saul said, "Who are you, Lord?"

The voice answered, "I am Jesus, whom you are persecuting. ⁶Get up now and go into the city. Someone there will tell you what you must do."

⁷The people traveling with Saul stood there but said nothing. They heard the voice, but they saw no one. ⁸Saul got up from the ground and opened his eyes, but he could not see. So those with Saul took his hand and led him into Damascus. ⁹For three days Saul could not see and did not eat or drink.

¹⁰There was a follower of Jesus in Damascus named Ananias. The Lord spoke to Ananias in a vision, "Ananias!"

Ananias answered, "Here I am, Lord."

¹¹The Lord said to him, "Get up and go to Straight Street. Find the house of Judas, and ask for a man named Saul from the city of Tarsus. He is there now, praying. ¹²Saul has seen a vision in which a man named Ananias comes to him and lays his hands on him. Then he is able to see again."

¹³But Ananias answered, "Lord, many people have told me about this man and the terrible things he did to your holy people in Jerusalem. ¹⁴Now he has come here to Damascus, and the leading priests have given him the power to arrest everyone who worships you."

¹⁵But the Lord said to Ananias, "Go! I have chosen Saul for an important work. He must tell about me to those who are not Jews, to kings, and to the people of Israel. ¹⁶I will show him how much he must suffer for my name."

¹⁷So Ananias went to the house of Judas. He laid his hands on Saul and said, "Brother Saul, the Lord Jesus sent me. He is the one you saw on the road on your way here. He sent me so that you can see again and be filled with the Holy Spirit." ¹⁸Immediately, something that looked like fish scales fell from Saul's eyes, and he was able to see again! Then Saul got up and was baptized. ¹⁹After he ate some food, his strength returned.

Saul stayed with the followers of Jesus in Damascus for a few days. ²⁰Soon he began to preach about Jesus in the synagogues, saying, "Jesus is the Son of God."

NKJV

³As he journeyed he came near Damascus, and suddenly a light shone around him from heaven. ⁴Then he fell to the ground, and heard a voice saying to him, "Saul, Saul, why are you persecuting Me?"

⁵And he said, "Who are You, Lord?"

Then the Lord said, "I am Jesus, whom you are persecuting. It is hard for you to kick against the goads."

⁶So he, trembling and astonished, said, "Lord, what do You want me to do?"

Then the Lord said to him, "Arise and go into the city, and you will be told what you must do."

⁷And the men who journeyed with him stood speechless, hearing a voice but seeing no one. ⁸Then Saul arose from the ground, and when his eyes were opened he saw no one. But they led him by the hand and brought him into Damascus. ⁹And he was three days without sight, and neither ate nor drank.

¹⁰Now there was a certain disciple at Damascus named Ananias; and to him the Lord said in a vision, "Ananias."

And he said, "Here I am, Lord."

¹¹So the Lord said to him, "Arise and go to the street called Straight, and inquire at the house of Judas for one called Saul of Tarsus, for behold, he is praying. ¹²And in a vision he has seen a man named Ananias coming in and putting his hand on him, so that he might receive his sight."

¹³Then Ananias answered, "Lord, I have heard from many about this man, how much harm he has done to Your saints in Jerusalem. ¹⁴And here he has authority from the chief priests to bind all who call on Your name."

¹⁵But the Lord said to him, "Go, for he is a chosen vessel of Mine to bear My name before Gentiles, kings, and the children of Israel. ¹⁶For I will show him how many things he must suffer for My name's sake."

¹⁷And Ananias went his way and entered the house; and laying his hands on him he said, "Brother Saul, the Lord Jesus, who appeared to you on the road as you came, has sent me that you may receive your sight and be filled with the Holy Spirit." ¹⁸Immediately there fell from his eyes something like scales, and he received his sight at once; and he arose and was baptized.

¹⁹So when he had received food, he was strengthened. Then Saul spent some days with the disciples at Damascus.

²⁰Immediately he preached the Christ in the synagogues, that He is the Son of God.

EXPLORATION

1. Whom did Saul meet on his way to Damascus? How?

Holy Spirit Jesus through a light from cheaven

2. What did the voice from heaven tell Saul about his past and his future?

Past. That he was presecuting Jesus
Future - People will tell you in the City of Damacus what to do

3. How long did Saul have to wait for further instructions from the Lord?

Until Ananias came 3 day Blind

4. How did Ananias minister to Saul?

With the help of the holy spirit he gave him his sight back & told him about Jesus

5. How was God's power revealed in Saul's life?

God took his sight & gave it back in Saul saw the light

INSPIRATION

Before he encountered Christ, Paul had been somewhat of a hero among the Pharisees . . . Blue-blooded and wild-eyed, this young zealot was hellbent on keeping the kingdom pure—and that meant keeping the Christians out. He marched through the countryside like a general demanding that backslidden Jews salute the flag of the motherland or kiss their family and hopes good-bye.

All this came to a halt, however, on the shoulder of a highway . . . That's when someone slammed on the stadium lights, and he heard the voice.

When he found out whose voice it was, his jaw hit the ground, and his body followed. He braced himself for the worst. He knew it was all over . . . He prayed that death would be quick and painless.

But all he got was silence and the first of a lifetime of surprises.

He ended up bewildered and befuddled in a borrowed bedroom. God left him there a few days with scales on his eyes so thick that the only direction he could look was inside himself. And he didn't like what he saw. He saw himself for what he really was—to use his own words, the worst of sinners . . . Alone in the room with his sins on his conscience and blood on his hands, he asked to be cleansed. The legalist Saul was buried, and the liberator Paul was born. He was never the same afterwards. And neither was the world.

The message is gripping: Show a man his failures without Jesus, and the result will be found in the roadside gutter. Give a man religion without reminding him of his filth, and the result will be arrogance in a three-piece suit. But get the two in the same heart—get sin to meet Savior and Savior to meet sin—and the result just might be another Pharisee turned preacher who sets the world on fire. (From *The Applause of Heaven* by Max Lucado)

REACTION

6. With which person in the story do you identify: Saul, his companions, or Ananias? Explain.

7. What does this passage teach us about God? About people?

8. Describe your conversion experience. Why is it helpful to share our stories with one another?

9. List some of the ways God can use us to minister to unbelievers.

10. Think of a time when God used you to minister to someone else. What did you do?

11. How can you minister to someone who has not yet experienced God's saving power?

LIFE LESSONS

Life can be a stunning mixture of "Saul" experiences and "Ananias" opportunities. Sometimes we're the target; sometimes we're the arrow. We are served; we serve. Because we are first loved and saved, we get wonderful chances to participate in the miracle of other people's life-change. On this side of eternity we're never far from attitudes and sin that cause God to treat us like Saul on the road to Damascus, nor far from moments when God calls us to step into Ananias's sandals in someone else's life.

DEVOTION

Father, when we think of what you have done for us, we feel only humble gratitude. We can never thank you enough for sacrificing your Son to save us. You rescued us from an eternity of suffering and offered us everlasting joy. We praise you, Father, for displaying your saving power in us.

For more Bible passages about God's power to save, see Psalm 68:20; Daniel 3:17; Zephaniah 3:17; Matthew 1:21; John 3:3–8, 16–21; 6:44, 65; Acts 22:14–16; Romans 10:9–13; Hebrews 7:25.

To complete the book of Acts during this twelve-part study, read Acts 9:1–43.

JOURNALING

How can I thank God for saving me? Who could be my human sounding board?

UNITY
AMONG
BELIEVERS

MAX
LUCADO

REFLECTION

We know that the church should be a place of unity and harmony, focusing on worshipping and honoring God. But all too often church groups fall into the "we/them" trap of disunity and discord. The early church, made up of Jewish believers, had these struggles too. God wanted to expand the boundaries to the Gentiles, and they weren't quite ready for that. Think about your own church body. Is it a place of unity? Why or why not? How do you think "outsiders" feel when they visit?

SITUATION

One of the first non-Jews to embrace the gospel was Cornelius, a Roman centurion stationed at Palestinian Caesarea. God gave separate visions to Cornelius and Peter to set the stage for their meeting and to show Peter that Gentiles were included in God's plan—a radical idea. Peter was waiting for Cornelius's invitation. He did not know who waited for him in the Gentile's house, but he was under orders to be there and offer whoever would listen the message of salvation.

OBSERVATION

Read Acts 10:24–25 from the NCV or the NKJV.

NCV

24On the following day they came to Caesarea. Cornelius was waiting for them and had called together his relatives and close friends. 25When Peter entered, Cornelius met him, fell at his feet, and worshiped him. 26But Peter helped him up, saying, "Stand up. I too am only a human." 27As he talked with Cornelius, Peter went inside where he saw many people gathered. 28He said, "You people understand that it is against our Jewish law for Jewish people to associate with or visit anyone who is not Jewish. But God has shown me that I should not call any person 'unholy' or 'unclean.' 29That is why I did not argue when I was asked to come here. Now, please tell me why you sent for me."

30Cornelius said, "Four days ago, I was praying in my house at this same time—three o'clock in the afternoon. Suddenly, there was a man standing before me wearing shining clothes. 31He said, 'Cornelius, God has heard your prayer and has seen that you give to the poor and remembers you. 32So send some men to Joppa and ask Simon Peter to come. Peter is staying in the house of a man, also named Simon, who is a tanner and has a house beside the sea.' 33So I sent for you immediately, and it was very good of you to come. Now we are all here before God to hear everything the Lord has commanded you to tell us."

34Peter began to speak: "I really understand now that to God every person is the same. 35In every country God accepts anyone who worships him and does what is right.

NKJV

24And the following day they entered Caesarea. Now Cornelius was waiting for them, and had called together his relatives and close friends. 25As Peter was coming in, Cornelius met him and fell down at his feet and worshiped him. 26But Peter lifted him up, saying, "Stand up; I myself am also a man." 27And as he talked with him, he went in and found many who had come together. 28Then he said to them, "You know how unlawful it is for a Jewish man to keep company with or go to one of another nation. But God has shown me that I should not call any man common or unclean. 29Therefore I came without objection as soon as I was sent for. I ask, then, for what reason have you sent for me?"

30So Cornelius said, "Four days ago I was fasting until this hour; and at the ninth hour I prayed in my house, and behold, a man stood before me in bright clothing, 31and said, 'Cornelius, your prayer has been heard, and your alms are remembered in the sight of God. 32Send therefore to Joppa and call Simon here, whose surname is Peter. He is lodging in the house of Simon, a tanner, by the sea. When he comes, he will speak to you.' 33So I sent to you immediately, and you have done well to come. Now therefore, we are all present before God, to hear all the things commanded you by God."

34Then Peter opened his mouth and said: "In truth I perceive that God shows no partiality. 35But in every nation whoever fears Him and works righteousness is accepted by Him."

EXPLORATION

1. How did Cornelius prepare for his meeting with Peter?

> He called his friend &
> relatives & waited for
> Peter - He sent men to
> get Peter.

2. Why was divine intervention necessary to bring Peter and Cornelius together?

> Because Peter was Jewish
> & Cornelius was an
> unclean gentile. Not
> a chosen one.

3. What lesson did God teach Peter? How?

> To That
> all people should be equal
> in the eyes of God.
> Peter had a vision - God told
> him to eat meat from a
> blanket of animals felt but Peter
> some where unclear

4. What did Cornelius want from Peter?

He was going to worship them but Peter set him straight —

5. How did Peter's vision change his view of God and others?

Peter's vision made him realize that all men are equal in the eyes of God. Anyone can worship God

INSPIRATION

How many pulpit hours have been wasted on preaching the trivial? How many churches have tumbled at the throes of minisculity? How many leaders have saddled their pet peeves, drawn their swords of bitterness and launched into battle against brethren over issues that are not worth discussing?

So close to the cross but so far from the Christ.

We specialize in "I am right" rallies. We write books about what the other does wrong. We major in finding gossip and become experts in unveiling weaknesses. We split into little huddles and then, God forbid, we split again . . .

Are our differences that divisive? Are our opinions that obtrusive? Are our walls that wide? Is it *that* impossible to find a common cause?

"May they all be one," Jesus prayed.

One. Not one in groups of two thousand. But one in One. One church. One faith. One Lord. Not Baptist, not Methodist, not Adventist. Just Christian. No denominations. No hierarchies. No traditions. Just Christ.

Too idealistic? Impossible to achieve? I don't think so. Harder things have been done, you know. For example, once upon a tree, a Creator gave his life for his creation. Maybe all we need are a few hearts that are willing to follow suit. (From *No Wonder They Call Him the Savior* by Max Lucado)

REACTION

6. What differences divide believers today?

Baptism

Communion

type of worship service

Personalities

7. What issues do you think Christians should not fight over? What issues are worth discussing?

That Christ came for us all.

Everything is worth discussing but no two people see the whole Bible the same —

8. What can we do to build a sense of unity in the church?

National day of prayer.
Truely except other —

9. Why is a lack of unity harmful to the church?

I'm right your wrong attitude.

10. How can believers remain unified when disagreements arise?

Listening to others doesn't mean agreement. But try to understand each others views

11. How can you help your Christian brothers and sisters focus on the common ground you share?

Start with Christ's love.

LIFE LESSONS

For followers of Jesus today, the unity issue boils down to how we welcome people into our circle, our fellowship. Are we quick to give forceful reasons why they shouldn't want to join us, or are we eager to invite them to follow Jesus with us as the Lord works out change in each of our lives? Peter had a message to deliver, but his presence among the Gentiles delivered a powerful illustration that his message was true. Let your presence do the same.

DEVOTION

Father, your heart must break when you see selfishness, competition, and discord in your church. Help us to take our eyes off ourselves so that we can focus on the common ground we share in you. Father, strengthen your church by filling us with your love.

For more Bible passages about Christian unity, see 2 Chronicles 30:12; Psalm 133:1; John 17:23; Romans 15:5; Ephesians 4:3–13; Philippians 2:1; Colossians 2:2; 3:14.

To complete the book of Acts during this twelve-part study, read Acts 10:1–13:52.

JOURNALING

If I have contributed to any division or discord in my church, what can I do to make things right?

Try not to not pick

L E S S O N   N I N E

GOD'S GRACE

MAX
LUCADO

REFLECTION

One of the ways we resist change is by creating traditions. Thoughtful traditions bring stability to life. But they can also create a rigid environment where desperately needed change cannot occur. This lesson will allow us to look at cherished tradition in the light of God's grace. We will think together about how God brings about change in people and in situations. What is one of your favorite religious traditions? Why?

SITUATION

Gentiles were turning to Christ by the scores. Soon, non-Jewish believers would outnumber the Jews in the church. For some of the early Jewish Christians, the situation was getting out of hand. One way to prevent that was to insist that everyone accept the rules and culture of Judaism as part of the requirement before their faith in Christ would be recognized. Paul and Barnabas insisted that such added regulations would complicate and undermine the gospel of Jesus Christ. The stakes were high. The church leaders in Jerusalem decided to bring the discussion to an official decision.

OBSERVATION

Read Acts 15:1–11 from the NCV or the NKJV.

NCV

¹*Then some people came to Antioch from Judea and began teaching the non-Jewish believers: "You cannot be saved if you are not circumcised as Moses taught us." ²Paul and Barnabas were against this teaching and argued with them about it. So the church decided to send Paul, Barnabas, and some others to Jerusalem where they could talk more about this with the apostles and elders.*

3The church helped them leave on the trip, and they went through the countries of Phoenicia and Samaria, telling all about how those who were not Jewish had turned to God. This made all the believers very happy. 4When they arrived in Jerusalem, they were welcomed by the apostles, the elders, and the church. Paul, Barnabas, and the others told about everything God had done with them. 5But some of the believers who belonged to the Pharisee group came forward and said, "The non-Jewish believers must be circumcised. They must be told to obey the law of Moses."

6The apostles and the elders gathered to consider this problem. 7After a long debate, Peter stood up and said to them, "Brothers, you know that in the early days God chose me from among you to preach the Good News to those who are not Jewish. They heard the Good News from me, and they believed. 8God, who knows the thoughts of everyone, accepted them. He showed this to us by giving them the Holy Spirit, just as he did to us. 9To God, those people are not different from us. When they believed, he made their hearts pure. 10So now why are you testing God by putting a heavy load around the necks of the non-Jewish believers? It is a load that neither we nor our ancestors were able to carry. 11But we believe that we and they too will be saved by the grace of the Lord Jesus."

NKJV

1And certain men came down from Judea and taught the brethren, "Unless you are circumcised according to the custom of Moses, you cannot be saved." 2Therefore, when Paul and Barnabas had no small dissension and dispute with them, they determined that Paul and Barnabas and certain others of them should go up to Jerusalem, to the apostles and elders, about this question.

3So, being sent on their way by the church, they passed through Phoenicia and Samaria, describing the conversion of the Gentiles; and they caused great joy to all the brethren. 4And when they had come to Jerusalem, they were received by the church and the apostles and the elders; and they reported all things that God had done with them. 5But some of the sect of the Pharisees who believed rose up, saying, "It is necessary to circumcise them, and to command them to keep the law of Moses."

6Now the apostles and elders came together to consider this matter. 7And when there had been much dispute, Peter rose up and said to them: "Men and brethren, you know that a good while ago God chose among us, that by my mouth the Gentiles should hear the word of the gospel and believe. 8So God, who knows the heart, acknowledged them by giving them the Holy Spirit, just as He did to us, 9and made no distinction between us and them, purifying their hearts by faith. 10Now therefore, why do you test God by putting a yoke on the neck of the disciples which neither our fathers nor we were able to bear? 11But we believe that through the grace of the Lord Jesus Christ we shall be saved in the same manner as they."

EXPLORATION

1. What controversy arose in this early church?

2. How did the Gentile believers decide to resolve the problem?

3. How did God show his acceptance of the Gentile Christians?

4. Why did Peter accuse some Pharisees of testing God?

5. What final statement did Peter make to the council about salvation?

INSPIRATION

God is not the God of confusion, and wherever he sees sincere seekers with confused hearts, you can bet your sweet December that he will do whatever it takes to help them see his will . . . His plan hasn't changed. Jesus still speaks to believers through believers. "The whole body depends on Christ, and all the parts of the body are joined and held together. Each part does its own work to make the whole body grow and be strong with love" (Eph. 4:16 NCV).

While I was driving to my office this morning, my eye saw a traffic light. The sensors within my eye perceived that the color of the light was red. My brain checked my memory bank and announced the meaning of a red light to my right foot. My right foot responded by leaving the accelerator and pressing the brake.

Now what if my body hadn't functioned properly? What if my eye had decided not to be a part of the body because the nose had hurt its feelings? Or what if the foot was tired of being bossed around and decided to press the gas pedal instead of the brake? Or what if the right foot was in pain, but too proud to tell the left foot, so the left foot didn't know to step in and help? In all instances, a wreck would occur.

God has given each part of the body of Christ an assignment. One way God reveals his will to you is through the church. He speaks to one member of his body through another member. It could happen in a Bible class, a small group, during communion, or during dessert. God has as many methods as he has people. (From *The Great House of God* by Max Lucado)

REACTION

6. How does the gracious attitude of Paul, Barnabas, and Peter challenge you?

7. What does it mean to extend God's grace to others?

8. Why is it difficult for some people to receive God's acceptance by grace?

9. What traditions or practices have some Christians added to the gospel?

10. How can we determine whether the requirements for faith taught in our churches are established by God or people?

11. How can we guard against expecting more of new Christians than God expects?

LIFE LESSONS

Some differences between Christians boil down to preferences. The early believers had to discover a way to settle these differences so that truthful and godly standards could remain but insignificant alternatives could be accepted. How do you react to Christians whose worship style is different from your own? Remember God's gift of eternal life is free and for everybody, whatever their color, race, or worship preference. Have the same gracious attitude toward others that Jesus had.

DEVOTION

Father, forgive us for the times we have insulted you by trying to earn your acceptance. And forgive us for putting heavy burdens on others who want to know you. We know that you save people, not because of what they have done, but because of your amazing grace.

For more Bible passages about grace, see John 1:16; Romans 3:23–24; 2 Corinthians 12:9; Galatians 2:15–21; Ephesians 2:4–9; 2 Thessalonians 2:16–17; 1 Timothy 1:14; Titus 3:4–7; Hebrews 12:15.

To complete the book of Acts during this twelve-part study, read Acts 14:1–16:40.

JOURNALING

How does this passage deepen my understanding of God's grace? What difference should this make in my daily life?

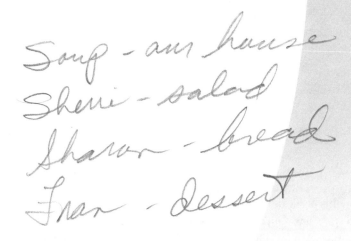

Feb –

LESSON TEN

PRESENTING
THE GOSPEL

Soup – our house
Sherri – salad
Sharon – bread
Fran – dessert

MAX
LUCADO

REFLECTION

Most of us instinctively avoid the direct approach of witnessing: "Brother, are you saved?" Some people can manage this approach without offending, but most of us settle for something more subtle. We want to connect with people. We desire to share, but with a reasonable expectation of gaining a hearing. What do you think attracts people to Christianity? What turns people away?

SITUATION

By this point in his missionary career, Paul was being greatly used by God to start new churches. His travels led him to the philosophical capital of the world—Athens. He wanted to gain a hearing among the intellectuals. As he walked through the city's market, he made an observation that stunned him. His opening became obvious. He would start with the history, culture, and traditions of his audience.

OBSERVATION

Read Acts 17:16–31 from the NCV or the NKJV.

NCV

[16]While Paul was waiting for Silas and Timothy in Athens, he was troubled because he saw that the city was full of idols. [17]In the synagogue, he talked with the Jews and the Greeks who worshiped God. He also talked every day with people in the marketplace.

[18]Some of the Epicurean and Stoic philosophers argued with him, saying, "This man doesn't know what he is talking about. What is he trying to say?" Others said, "He seems to be telling us about some other gods," because Paul was telling them about Jesus and his rising from the dead. [19]They got Paul and took him to a meeting of the Areopagus, where they said, "Please explain to us this new idea you have been teaching. [20]The things you are saying are new to us, and we want to know what this teaching means." [21](All the people of Athens and those from other countries who lived there always used their time to talk about the newest ideas.)

[22]Then Paul stood before the meeting of the Areopagus and said, "People of Athens, I can see you are very religious in all things. [23]As I was going through your city, I saw the objects you worship. I found an altar that had these words written on it: TO A GOD WHO IS NOT KNOWN. You worship a god that you don't know, and this is the God I am telling you about! [24]The God who made the whole world and everything in it is the Lord of the land and the sky. He does not live in temples built by human hands. [25]This God is the One who gives life, breath, and everything else to people. He does not need any help from them; he has everything he needs. [26]God began by making one person, and from him came all the different people who live everywhere in the world. God decided exactly when and where they must live. [27]God wanted them to look for him and perhaps search all around for him and find him, though he is not far from any of us: [28]'We live in him. We walk in him. We are in him.' Some of your own poets have said: 'For we are his children.' [29]Since we are God's children, you must not think that God is like something that people imagine or make from gold, silver, or rock. [30]In the past, people did not understand God, and he ignored this. But now, God tells all people in the world to change their hearts and lives. [31]God has set a day that he will judge all the world with fairness, by the man he chose long ago. And God has proved this to everyone by raising that man from the dead!"

NKJV

[16]Now while Paul waited for them at Athens, his spirit was provoked within him when he saw that the city was given over to idols. [17]Therefore he reasoned in the synagogue with the Jews and with the Gentile worshipers, and in the marketplace daily with those who happened to be there. [18]Then certain Epicurean and Stoic philosophers encountered him. And some said, "What does this babbler want to say?"

Others said, "He seems to be a proclaimer of foreign gods," because he preached to them Jesus and the resurrection.

¹⁹*And they took him and brought him to the Areopagus, saying, "May we know what this new doctrine is of which you speak? ²⁰For you are bringing some strange things to our ears. Therefore we want to know what these things mean." ²¹For all the Athenians and the foreigners who were there spent their time in nothing else but either to tell or to hear some new thing.*

²²*Then Paul stood in the midst of the Areopagus and said, "Men of Athens, I perceive that in all things you are very religious; ²³for as I was passing through and considering the objects of your worship, I even found an altar with this inscription:*

TO THE UNKNOWN GOD.

Therefore, the One whom you worship without knowing, Him I proclaim to you: ²⁴God, who made the world and everything in it, since He is Lord of heaven and earth, does not dwell in temples made with hands. ²⁵Nor is He worshiped with men's hands, as though He needed anything, since He gives to all life, breath, and all things. ²⁶And He has made from one blood every nation of men to dwell on all the face of the earth, and has determined their preappointed times and the boundaries of their dwellings, ²⁷so that they should seek the Lord, in the hope that they might grope for Him and find Him, though He is not far from each one of us; ²⁸for in Him we live and move and have our being, as also some of your own poets have said, 'For we are also His offspring.' ²⁹Therefore, since we are the offspring of God, we ought not to think that the Divine Nature is like gold or silver or stone, something shaped by art and man's devising. ³⁰Truly, these times of ignorance God overlooked, but now commands all men everywhere to repent, ³¹because He has appointed a day on which He will judge the world in righteousness by the Man whom He has ordained. He has given assurance of this to all by raising Him from the dead."

EXPLORATION

1. What motivated Paul to preach the gospel in Athens?

He saw a city full of Idols

2. Why were the people interested in Paul's message?

It was a new idea to them

3. How did Paul use his knowledge of the culture to present his case to the Council?

He talked about the altar to a God who is unknown

4. How did Paul explain that the true God is different from other gods?

He real not a piece of art or an idol. He doesn't need us — He created the world + life

5. What has God proven to everyone? How?

That he is fair by raising Christ from the dead.

INSPIRATION

It's not God's plan for your heart to roam as a Bedouin. God wants you to move in out of the cold and live . . . with him. Under his roof there is space available. At his table a plate is set. In his living room a wingback chair is reserved just for you. And he'd like you to take up residence in his house. Why would he want you to share his home?

Simple, he's your Father.

You were intended to live in your Father's house. Any place less than his is insufficient. Any place far from his is dangerous. Only the home built for your heart can protect your heart. And your Father wants you to dwell *in* him.

No, you didn't misread the sentence and I didn't miswrite it. Your Father doesn't ask you to live *with* him, he asks you to live *in* him. As Paul wrote, "For in him we live and move and have our being" (Acts 17:28 NIV).

Don't think you are separated from God, he at the top end of a great ladder, you at the other. Dismiss any thought that God is on Venus while you are on earth. Since God is Spirit (John 4:23), he is next to you: God himself is our wall. And God himself is our foundation. . . .

For many this is a new thought. We think of God as a deity to discuss, not a place to dwell. We think of God as a mysterious miracle worker, not a house to live in. We think of God as a creator to call on, not a home to reside in. But our Father wants to be much more. He wants to be the one in whom "we live and move and have our being" (Acts 17:28 NIV).

Heaven knows no difference between Sunday morning and Wednesday afternoon. God longs to speak as clearly in the workplace as he does in the sanctuary.
He longs to be worshipped when we sit at the dinner table and not just when
we come to his communion table. You may go days without thinking of him, but
there's not a moment when he's not thinking of you. (From *The Great House of God*
by Max Lucado)

REACTION

6. How does the fact that God dwells in you give you courage to speak out about
Him?

7. What can we copy from Paul's methods when we share our faith with others?

Remember who we're talking to & relate our faith to their interests.

8. What is the danger in changing our approach and presentation to fit our audience?

Is it from the scripture?

9. What points should you include while sharing the gospel with non-Christians?

God's love — He came & died for everyone —

10. What happens when Christians assume that everyone has the same perspective and background? List several cultural factors that you think Christians should consider in their evangelistic efforts.

11. What are some ways you can share the gospel with coworkers or friends?

Just make church sound [strikethrough] important in your life.

LIFE LESSONS

One of the great lessons we can take from Paul's experience in Athens has to do with his practice of observing people. He looked for clues to their life-quests. What people were involved in often revealed what they were looking for, even if they didn't realize it. Believers who become lovingly observant of people around them discover all kinds of opportunities and open doors for sharing their faith. Meanwhile, a believer's life ought to also provoke questions like, "Why are you so hopeful in your outlook?" (see 1 Peter 3:15).

DEVOTION

Father, we cannot communicate the truth of the gospel without your help. Take our fears and inadequacies and use them to advance your kingdom. Give us your heart for the lost, your compassion for the hurting, and your wisdom for the troubled. Speak through us to draw people to yourself.

For more Bible passages about witnessing, see Acts 1:8; Romans 1:14–16; 15:15–20; 1 Corinthians 1:17; 9:16–18; 1 Thessalonians 2:4–13; 2 Timothy 4:2–5.

To complete the book of Acts during this twelve-part study, read Acts 17:1–20:16.

JOURNALING

What is keeping me from effectively sharing my testimony with others? How can I begin to eliminate those hindrances?

FACING PROBLEMS AND PAIN

MAX LUCADO

REFLECTION

Pain, difficulty, and struggles always feel and look different when they invade our lives. The responses we expect from others seem harder for us to practice. If we haven't decided beforehand how we will view problems, they will dictate our responses. God's Word gives us a number of examples of people who faced over-whelming difficulties. We can learn from them. Think of a time when you have seen someone display joy or courage even through suffering. How do you think that person was able to be joyful or courageous?

SITUATION

As his third missionary journey was winding down, Paul still had many objec-tives he wanted to accomplish (such as visiting Spain). Yet he became aware that his time for ministry was coming to an end. He was on the way to Jerusalem and expected that events would lead him in a radical new direction. He gathered the Ephesians elders and leaders to give them some parting words.

OBSERVATION

Read Acts 27:13–25 in the NCV or the NKJV.

NCV

17Now from Miletus Paul sent to Ephesus and called for the elders of the church. 18When they came to him, he said, "You know about my life from the first day I came to Asia. You know the way I lived all the time I was with you. 19The Jews made plans against me, which troubled me very much. But you know I always served the Lord unselfishly, and I often cried. 20You know I preached to you and did not hold back anything that would help you. You know that I taught you in public and in your homes. 21I warned both Jews and Greeks to change their lives and turn to God and believe in our Lord Jesus. 22But now I must obey the Holy Spirit and go to Jerusalem. I don't know what will happen to me there. 23I know only that in every city the Holy Spirit tells me that troubles and even jail wait for me. 24I don't care about my own life. The most important thing is that I complete my mission, the work that the Lord Jesus gave me—to tell people the Good News about God's grace.

25 "And now, I know that none of you among whom I was preaching the kingdom of God will ever see me again. 26So today I tell you that if any of you should be lost, I am not responsible, 27because I have told you everything God wants you to know. 28Be careful for yourselves and for all the people the Holy Spirit has given to you to care for. You must be like shepherds to the church of God, which he bought with the death of his own son. 29I know that after I leave, some people will come like wild wolves and try to destroy the flock. 30Also, some from your own group will rise up and twist the truth and will lead away followers after them. 31So be careful! Always remember that for three years, day and night, I never stopped warning each of you, and I often cried over you.

NKJV

17From Miletus he sent to Ephesus and called for the elders of the church. 18And when they had come to him, he said to them: "You know, from the first day that I came to Asia, in what manner I always lived among you, 19serving the Lord with all humility, with many tears and trials which happened to me by the plotting of the Jews; 20how I kept back nothing that was helpful, but proclaimed it to you, and taught you publicly and from house to house, 21testifying to Jews, and also to Greeks, repentance toward God and faith toward our Lord Jesus Christ. 22And see, now I go bound in the spirit to Jerusalem, not knowing the things that will happen to me there, 23except that the Holy Spirit testifies in every city, saying that chains and tribulations await me. 24But none of these things move me; nor do I count my life dear to myself, so that I may finish my race with joy, and the ministry which I received from the Lord Jesus, to testify to the gospel of the grace of God.

²⁵ "And indeed, now I know that you all, among whom I have gone preaching the kingdom of God, will see my face no more. ²⁶Therefore I testify to you this day that I am innocent of the blood of all men. ²⁷For I have not shunned to declare to you the whole counsel of God. ²⁸Therefore take heed to yourselves and to all the flock, among which the Holy Spirit has made you overseers, to shepherd the church of God which He purchased with His own blood. ²⁹For I know this, that after my departure savage wolves will come in among you, not sparing the flock. ³⁰Also from among yourselves men will rise up, speaking perverse things, to draw away the disciples after themselves. ³¹Therefore watch, and remember that for three years I did not cease to warn everyone night and day with tears.

EXPLORATION

1. Why did Paul ask the church elders to meet him in Miletus?

2. How was Paul tested during his ministry in Asia?

3. How did the Holy Spirit work in Paul's life?

4. What was Paul's attitude toward the hardships he faced?

5. What was Paul's goal in life?

INSPIRATION

As you think about [hardships], how do you explain yours? The tension at home. The demands at work. The bills on your desk or the tumor in your body. You aren't taken hostage, but aren't you occasionally taken aback by God's silence? He knows what you are facing. How do we explain this?

Maybe God messed up. Cancer cells crept into your DNA when he wasn't looking. He was so occupied with the tornado in Kansas that he forgot the famine in Uganda. He tried to change the stubborn streak in your spouse but just couldn't get him to budge. Honestly. A bumbling Creator? An absent-minded Maker? What evidence does Scripture provide to support such a view? What evidence does creation offer? Can't the Maker of heaven and earth handle bad traffic and prevent bad marriages? Of course he can. Then why doesn't he?

Perhaps he is mad. Have we so exhausted the mercy of God's bank account that every prayer bounces like a bad check? Did humanity cross the line millenniums ago, and now we're getting what we deserve? Such an argument carries a dash of merit. God does leave us to the consequences of our stupid decisions. Think of Egyptian soldiers in Red Sea, Hebrews in Babylon, Peter weeping with the sound of a crowing rooster in his ears. Bang your heard against the wall, and expect a headache. God lets us endure the fruit of sin. But to label him peeved and impatient? To do so you need to scissor from your Bible some tender passages such as: "God is sheer mercy and grace; not easily angered, he's rich in love. He doesn't endlessly nag and scold, nor hold grudges forever. He doesn't treat us as our sins deserve, nor pay us back in full for our wrongs. As high as heaven is over the earth, so strong is his love to those who fear him" (Ps. 103:8–11 MSG).

Don't blame suffering in the world on the anger of God. He's not mad; he didn't mess up. Follow our troubles to their headwaters, and you won't find an angry or befuddled God. But you will find a sovereign God.

Your pain has a purpose. Your problems, struggles, heartaches, and hassles cooperate toward one end—the glory of God. "Trust me in your times of trouble, and I will rescue you, and you will give me glory" (Ps. 50:15 NLT). Not an easy assignment to swallow. Not for you. Not for me. (From *It's Not About Me* by Max Lucado)

REACTION

6. Why is it important to recognize that pain is inevitable?

Pain is a warning sign
that something wrong

7. How do some people make their problems worse?

By blaming someone else
or not seeing the
problem as theirs

8. How can the Holy Spirit help us through life's difficulties?

Listen — to the
direction he give
us

9. Why do we try to handle our pain and problems on our own?

No one wants to ask for the help of others. We are showing our weakness or bothering someone with our problems.

10. What lessons has God taught you through the hardships you have endured?

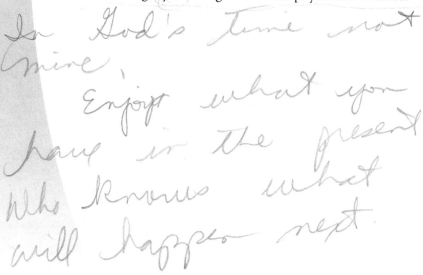

In God's time not mine.

Enjoy what you have in the present. Who knows what will happen next.

11. How does this passage challenge you to deal with your present problems?

LIFE LESSONS

In his wisdom, God seldom lets us know what will happen and how bad it may be. He tells us to trust him with all the arrangements. Our tendencies may always drift toward self-pity and questions, but God's Spirit will draw us back toward the truth. Every day becomes a new opportunity to discover in just how many different ways "it isn't about us." Life is about God's purposes and plans.

DEVOTION

Father, you promised that there would be faith and strength and hope to meet life's problems. Give that strength to those whose anxieties have buried their dreams, whose illnesses have hospitalized their hopes, whose burdens are bigger than their shoulders.

For more Bible passages about facing pain and problems, see Job 33:19–26; Psalm 34:19; Acts 5:41–42; Romans 5:3–4; 2 Corinthians 1:4–7; 4:17–18; 6:4–10; 2 Thessalonians 1:4–5; James 1:2–4; 1 Peter 1:6–7; 2:19–21; 4:12–16.

To complete the book of Acts during this twelve-part study, read Acts 20:17–24:23.

JOURNALING

What burdens are weighing me down? How can I release those problems to God?

LIVING YOUR FAITH

MAX LUCADO

REFLECTION

Faith seems to shine out when we experience times that are challenging or disastrous. But do we have to wait until something difficult occurs before we find out whether our faith is effective? What are some ways we can flex our faith muscles on ordinary days?

SITUATION

Paul's life was in God's hands. He had already faced death many times and fully expected to die in God's service in some way. His plans to visit Rome had taken a long detour but were coming to pass. Then disaster struck. He and his companions, along with their guards, were stuck on a ship in a life-threatening storm. Be sure to read how the adventure turns out, once you've studied this passage of men under extreme danger.

OBSERVATION

Read Acts 27:13–25 from the NCV or the NKJV.

NCV

13When a good wind began to blow from the south, the men on the ship thought, "This is the wind we wanted, and now we have it." So they pulled up the anchor, and we sailed very close to the island of Crete. 14But then a very strong wind named the "northeaster" came from the island. 15The ship was caught in it and could not sail against it. So we stopped trying and let the wind carry us. 16When we went below a small island named Cauda, we were barely able to bring in the lifeboat. 17After the men took the lifeboat in, they tied ropes around the ship to hold it together. The men were afraid that the ship would hit the sandbanks of Syrtis, so they lowered the sail and let the wind carry the ship. 18The next day the storm was blowing us so hard that the men threw out some of the cargo. 19A day later with their own hands they threw out the ship's equipment. 20When we could not see the sun or the stars for many days, and the storm was very bad, we lost all hope of being saved.

21After the men had gone without food for a long time, Paul stood up before them and said, "Men, you should have listened to me. You should not have sailed from Crete. Then you would not have all this trouble and loss. 22But now I tell you to cheer up because none of you will die. Only the ship will be lost. 23Last night an angel came to me from the God I belong to and worship. 24The angel said, 'Paul, do not be afraid. You must stand before Caesar. And God has promised you that he will save the lives of everyone sailing with you.' 25So men, have courage. I trust in God that everything will happen as his angel told me.

NKJV

13When the south wind blew softly, supposing that they had obtained their desire, putting out to sea, they sailed close by Crete. 14But not long after, a tempestuous head wind arose, called Euroclydon. 15So when the ship was caught, and could not head into the wind, we let her drive. 16And running under the shelter of an island called Clauda, we secured the skiff with difficulty. 17When they had taken it on board, they used cables to undergird the ship; and fearing lest they should run aground on the Syrtis Sands, they struck sail and so were driven. 18And because we were exceedingly tempest-tossed, the next day they lightened the ship. 19On the third day we threw the ship's tackle overboard with our own hands. 20Now when neither sun nor stars appeared for many days, and no small tempest beat on us, all hope that we would be saved was finally given up.

21But after long abstinence from food, then Paul stood in the midst of them and said, "Men, you should have listened to me, and not have sailed from Crete and incurred this disaster and loss. 22And now I urge you to take heart, for there will be no loss of life among you, but only of the ship. 23For there stood by me this night an angel of the God to whom I belong and whom I serve, 24saying, 'Do not be afraid, Paul; you must be brought before Caesar; and indeed God has granted you all those who sail with you.' 25Therefore take heart, men, for I believe God that it will be just as it was told me.

EXPLORATION

1. What life-threatening situation did Paul face on his way to Rome?

2. When did the people on board the ship lose hope of surviving?

3. How did Paul demonstrate his faith in God in the midst of a seemingly hopeless situation?

4. Why did Paul reprimand the men on the boat?

5. How did Paul encourage everyone while warning them of the danger ahead?

INSPIRATION

"Surely goodness and mercy shall follow me all the days of my life; and I will dwell in the house of the Lord forever" (Ps. 23:6 NKJV). This must be one of the sweetest phrases ever penned . . .

To read this verse is to open a box of jewels. Each word sparkles and begs to be examined in the face of our doubts: goodness, mercy, all the days, dwell in the house of the Lord, forever. They sweep in on insecurities like a SWAT team on a terrorist . . .

Our moods may shift, but God's doesn't. Our minds may change, but God's doesn't. Our devotion may falter, but God's never does. Even if we are faithless, he is faithful, for he cannot deny himself (see 2 Timothy 2:13). He is a sure God. And because he is a sure God, we can state confidently, "Surely goodness and mercy shall follow me all the days of my life."

Goodness and mercy will follow the child of God each and every day! Think of the days that lie ahead. What do you see? Days at home with only toddlers? God will be at your side. Days in a dead-end job? He will walk you through. Days of loneliness? He will take your hand. Surely goodness and mercy shall follow me—not some, not most, not nearly all—but all the days of my life . . . Isn't this the kind of God described in the Bible? A God who follows us? (From *Traveling Light* by Max Lucado)

REACTION

6. How is God's faithfulness related to our faith and confidence?

7. In what ways would you like to be more like Paul? Why?

8. What does it mean to live out your faith?

9. How does a hypocritical Christian impact others in the church and outside of the church?

10. How can we remind ourselves that people are watching the way we live?

11. What evidence of faith can others see in your life?

LIFE LESSONS

The book of Acts doesn't really end here. The record ceases, but the acts of the disciples go on, down through the ages. Just as Jesus promised, the fragile group of men and women that gathered in Jerusalem had been given power to become effective witnesses, sometimes even against their wishes. They left a legacy of faith for us to live out and pass on. No matter what circumstances Paul found himself in, he knew God was with him, following him every step. It was his role to run the race and keep the faith by sharing it with others. God wants to work in us and through us even when the storms and shipwrecks of life come. What kinds of "acts of disciples" will your chapter in God's story include?

DEVOTION

Without you, Father, we know it is impossible to live righteously. So we ask you to come alongside us and give us the strength to live what we believe. Help us to stand out as beacons of light in this dark world.

For more Bible passages about living your faith, see Galatians 2:20; Colossians 1:10; 1 Thessalonians 4:1–7; 2 Thessalonians 1:11; 1 Timothy 6:11–12; 2 Timothy 3:14–15; 4:7; Titus 2:11–14; Hebrews 4:14; James 2:14–24; 1 Peter 5:8–9.

To complete the book of Acts during this twelve-part study, read Acts 24:24–28:31.

JOURNALING

How do I usually react when things go wrong in my life? What can I do differently in the future to demonstrate my faith in God?

Lucado Life
Lesson Series

Revised and updated, the Lucado Life Lessons series is perfect for small group or individual use and includes intriguing questions that will take you deeper into God's Word.

Available at your local Christian Bookstore.